Karen Manzo
Rt.#1 Box 188-B
Rivesville, WV 26588

Smaller Than God

words of spiritual longing

Smaller Than God

words of spiritual longing

selected and edited by
Brother Paul Quenon and John B. Lee

Black Moss Press
2001

©2001 Copyright John B. Lee, Paul Quenon

Published by Black Moss Press at 2450 Byng Road, Windsor, Ontario, Canada N8W 3E8. Black Moss books are distributed in Canada and the U.S. by Firefly Books.

Black Moss would like to acknowledge the generous support of the Canada Council for the Arts and the Ontario Arts Council for its publishing program.

Acknowledgements

The Rienzi Crusz poem "Small Martyrdoms" from *Insurgent Rain: Selected Poems 1974-1996* (TSAR 1997) is reprinted here by the permission of the author.

The Al Purdy poem "Funeral" from *A Handful of Earth* (Black Moss Press, 1977) is reprinted by permission of Black Moss Press.

Cover photograph of Br. Paul Quenon by Marty Gervais

Table of Contents

Confessions (One) Degan Davis   11

A Legend Thomas Merton   11

Going Home Marty Gervais   13

I Wait Lea Harper   14

Go, Gather Up the Love Robert Priest   15

Sharing in Divinity Michael J. Wilson   16

A Meditation Between Claims Robyn Sarah   17

Landlord Lamentations Dale Ritterbusch   18

Advent Carols Frank Pool   19

Night Gone the Shadow of God John B. Lee   20

Poem for the Crew of the Kursk Erin Noteboom   22

Taking the Blame Robert Wynne   23

With the Heater on Robert Hilles   23

Death of the Black Cat Bruce Hunter   23

The Gift Dianne Aprile   27

Reversing a Crater Margaret Avison   29

Siesta George Whipple   33

Paying Attention John B. Lee   33

Crossing The Winter Fields James Deahl   35

Finding the Church Tony Cosier   36

Ernesto Cardenal   36

If Death Hovers Anywhere Grace Butcher   37

Names of Yahweh Marianne Bluger   38

Winterized Steven Michael Berzensky   38

desire for a different blue Julie Berry   39

Clothesline sonnet Roger Bell   39

"Thanksgiving" James Arthur   40

Unexpected beauty Roger Bell   41

earth remembers Julie Berry   42

Poem for a Winter's Night Robert Currie   43

Paths Laurie Smith   43

If I Were But a River Watching John B. Lee   43

Ode To The Letter P Richard E. Sherwin   47

An Island Where Evening Never Comes Liliana Ursu   49

Hymn of the Harrows 50

Psalm 139 tr.by Paul Quenon & Ned Rosebaum 50

A Psalm of Praise Jeff Seffinga 52

Psalm Marilyn Gear Pilling 53

Pater Ignatius Marianne Micros 54

God Forbid Bob Hill 56

Prayerful lies Marty Gervais 57

the singing Misha Felgin 58

The Blue Oats 59

Prayer On Leaving The Body James Deahl 60

Ernesto Cardenal 61

Just Before Christmas Barry Butson 62

Grace Marianne Bluger 63

In the Chapel Bernadette Dieker 64

Flight Liliana Ursu 64

Varieties of Religious Experience Peter Stevens 65

A Blessing Michael Henson 70

Theologians Never Ask the Obvious Robert Wynne 75

Adam's Rib Robert Hilles 75

Faith, 1998 Barry Dempster 77

Christ is the Kind of Guy Robert Priest 78

Department Store Jesus James Reaney 80

Last Suppers in Texas Linda Frank 82

Prime Mover Maurice Manning 83

Nuevo Laredo, Mexico Dorothy Mahoney 84

The Chair of Angels John B. Lee 85

Reading Revelation Sarah Klassen 87

He Couldn't Fix The Tractor Marty Gervais 88

the word Misha Felgin 90

Poor Man's Heaven Steven Michael Berzensky 91

Small Martyrdoms Rienzi Crusz 93

Perhaps Marty Roger Bell 95

Ernesto Cardenal 95

Tides Nelson Ball 95

God is in the Cracks Robert Sward 99

Acolytes Dale Ritterbusch 100

Bones of Desire Paul Quenon   100

The Christ of Velazquez Miguel de Unamuno   103

Funeral Al Purdy   104

Getting Close to God Robert Priest   105

The Farmers' Chapel Marty Gervais   106

Soul Purification William Robertson   109

Something More Miraculous Don Gutteridge   110

The Rapture Lea Harper   110

Chosen People Jeff Seffinga   112

Herzliyah Pituah Richard E. Sherwin   113

At the Support Group for Non-Believers Robert Wynne   116

The Agnostic's Villanelle Marilyn Taylor   117

Confessions (Two) Degan Davis   118

Part I

Soul Searching

Confessions (One)

Degan Davis

I went into the forest
and put my hand out
to the birds
like a perch

I had no peanuts or seed
but one landed
though I held
nothing

I have often worn myself
loudly
to the forest and the
city
walked through streets
like an accomplishment

I want to give you
nothing
but my hand

and for you
to take it

A Legend

Thomas Merton

They wanted to find Him
Their own way
They were willing
To let Him help;
But they were not willing
(Not at all willing)
To let anyone
Push them around.
Oh, they'd let them

Push them around
At the jute mills
And in the armies
And in the subway;
But they wouldn't
Let anyone push them
Around under the pretext
Of helping them.

And so a lot of people
Particularly the professional
Helpers of man,
Got to hate them.

There was nothing
They could do about it:
They were used to being hated:
It was where the whole
Trouble began.

But they wanted
To find Him
In their
Own way:
They wouldn't take anybody
Else's word
As final:
They would grope,
But they would find Him;
And gropingly
They did.

Going Home

Marty Gervais

The mist over the monastery
its white walls faded
into the haze
the sun just peeking
over the stiff steeple
see the cemetery
I wade into wet grass
My feet wet and
cold, think of a summer
morning in my youth
when I crossed a field
with a friend
a night of carousing
our eyes burning with
the new day, our
mouths tired from
so much laughing
our pant legs
soaked from the tall
weeds as we made
our way to the highway
always heading home
And today I stand on this
hill, see the outline of
the church emerging
like the face of a
saint forming in
the hands of a god
I see myself, a face
full of hope, believing in
the future, believing
in joy – yet
forever suspicious
forever confused
forever going
home

I Wait

Lea Harper

Between the potency and the existence
Between the essence and the descent...
                              —T.S.Eliot

I wait for you   *Ti aspetto.*   pregnant
like a swimmer   with anticipation
poised on the starting block
waits
in the protracted moment
before the gun goes off

I wait for you like a songbird
folded in silence
waits
for the first sign of morning

I wait for you
like a woman
in the agony of labour
waits for delivery

I wait for you
like Moses waited
for the voice of thunder
the tablet of truth
like poets wait
for the words
that will redeem them

I wait for you like the dying wait   Bapchia 3/08
for numbness to wash over them   Dad   9/08
for the ice flow to reach the heart
transcendent light enter the head
and The One they have always waited for
to come

My dear Jeanette 1/08

Do I call you angel of possibility
potency contained within perfection
the coupling of will and acquiescence?

14

Do I name you mercy
for which there is no metaphor
for which kindness and charity are
mere paltry human equivalents?
Or destiny, like God
from which there is no escape?
I have only a lover's impetus
toward union with the unknown creation
I am drawn
flesh to sword
moth to flame
for grace
and consummation

Aspetto.
Aspettero.
Ho aspettato.

Go, Gather Up the Love

Robert Priest

Go, gather up the love
I know now what we must do
It is in your eyes and my eyes
Go, and gather it up, look by look,
gaze by gaze,
one flame in hand, one holy flame-
two flames gathered up-
Gather it through slum and hovel
through mansion and factory
with great gentleness, go
taking a spark here a glow there
turning none of it
Gather it up and free it
if even just in your own lips
through your own heart
by being strong
by going always beyond your limits
Gather it to saturation
long past your centre
deeper than the full depth of you
Gather it up in beads
in blue flames, in fierce bonfires

15

in blue flames, in fierce bonfires
Let there be a leap of love
in the centre of the earth
a flame higher than the heavens
a leap of our commitment
of our will
a leap of fire
straight into the stars

Sharing in Divinity

Michael J. Wilson

once i was you
or will be
in the mystical body

but for now i am
michael joseph john wilson

once you were me
or will be

in the grand analysis
we knew each other
and interchanged

i will know you woman
as a woman
you will know me woman
as a man

in this way i am every sin
every wounded soul
every wounding of the soul

every worship every act of love
every disconnected thought
every ingestion

and just when i think i'm almost complete
it is our time to sprout

A Meditation Between Claims

Robyn Sarah

You want to close your hand
on something perfect, you want to say
Aha. Everything moves towards this,
or seems to move, you measure it
in the inches you must let down
on the children's overalls,
tearing the pages off the wall
each month; a friend phones
with news that another friend
has taken Tibetan vows, meanwhile the
kitchen is filling up with the smell
of burnt rice, you remind yourself
to buy postage stamps tomorrow

The mover
and the thing moved, are they two
or one; if two, is the thing moved
within or without, questions
you do not often bother yourself with
though you should; the corner store
is closed for the high holy days,
and though the air has a smell
not far from snow, your reluctance
to strip the garden is understandable

Laundry is piling up
in the back room, Mondays and Thursdays
the trash must be carried out
or it accumulates, each day
things get moved about and
put back in their places
and you accept this, the shape
that it gives a life, though the need
to make room supercedes other needs

If, bidding your guest goodbye,
you stand too long at the open door,
house-heat escapes, and the oil bill
will be higher next month, the toll
continues, wrapping the green tomatoes
in the news of the latest assassination.
The mover
and the thing moved, it all
comes down to this; one wants
to sit in the sun like a stone,
one wants to move the stone; which
is better

Landlord Lamentations

Dale Ritterbusch

The tenant downstairs
says Carlos is in the Spanish Mafia.
They deal drugs and scrawl graffiti
under the bridge outside of town.
Even when she's home
the woman across the hall
double locks her door,
ignores what she hears, what she sees.
Carlos complains about the lack of heat,
leaves the windows open all winter
so the smoke, the smell of grass, will dissipate.
On the night before he skips
he pushes his girlfriend down the stairs —

a baluster breaks; the girl cries.
He tells her he has other girlfriends, many;
she must understand, as we all must,
finally, in the end. I listen to the stories
the other tenants tell me,
imagine their lives, his life, what
it means to live like that. If I understood
any of this I would be someone else,
someone in a different life; what would I learn,
what would I know? I could repent
a life like that, and my repentance
would lift the sorrow of the world.
I clean the walls of his apartment, fill
chinks in the plaster, like bullet holes,
find the face of Jesus in a stain
bleeding down the walls. Jesus is in tears;
we're both in tears. We all want
the same thing: to look into the face of God
without shame, to earn eternal salvation, to get the rent
every month, always paid on time.

Advent Carols

Frank Pool

The old music gathers itself
in rehearsal, insistent
and familiar as the taste of
blood on the lips,
and the voices rise
in conspiracy and inspiration,
confined in the darkest
nights of the year.

You have withdrawn yourself
from me; I seek lost years
and test my pitch and tone
against the dark. The melody
is adequate to the ear, but
impotent in the heart. The

words take measure;   the soul
takes rest,

Time may help; the
wheel of birth beckons,
starry chariots of messages
and messengers to the past,
to the beloved dead, to the
eternal present   but time
makes evasive promises
ephemeral as song.

I have no sense of you
near me, yet my mind
and what is profounder than
mind are your willing
captives. I sing because
I can do nothing else; I wait
the advent of your return
lost in hope, not daring despair.

Night Gone the Shadow of God

John B. Lee

When Mark turned grey at eleven o'clock
on the dressing room bench
his skin lamping out
like an autumn salamander
next to a stone in the rain
we knew his distress
and I saw of a sudden
that these were good men
"lie down,"
one said with a knowing concern
"take off your shoes—
are you sick?"
and they gathered around
one rubbing his legs like a lover laughing
a little, one feeling the blue dab of his pulse

for slow sewing
watching his face
for poor maps of the heart
and the room
went round in well-meant jests
as a few of us stood
in the ill
circles of seen light
regarding his fear

"is he dying—I've seen men die
like that...
last year we lost a few"
the ice man says
and he breathes from the sad
deep wells of himself
to recall.

And though we'd played well
yet here we were now
with night gone
the shadow of God
and Mark on the bench
lying down
his eyelids like weeds in the wind
"I can't feel myself," he says
seeing something other than us.

November 10, 1999

Poem for the Crew of the Kursk

Erin Noteboom

*The submarine Kursk went to the bottom of the Barnets Sea, north
o Norway, on August 12th, 2000, and was declared lost after a
week of failed rescue efforts, on August 21st.*
Sunday, August 19th, 2000

I drive into the city before dawn, the grey rising
to silver, not yet pink. It's Saturday, and no one is up,
only a farmer in a John Deere cap coming in to market,
truckers hunched over coffee in a golden donut shop.
In the engineering building the only living thing
is a sparrow that must have flown through the loading dock.
She is against the wall, now, at the deep
and narrow windows. She strikes the glass, her wings
churning. She sinks and rests. She lifts
and strikes. I go to the lab and set the vacuum chamber
pumping down. The tanks hiss and the pipes clunk
and the whole time the sparrow makes the cry
that is called singing. When I can leave the apparatus
I go back. Battered and tied to the light,
the sparrow is easy to catch. I hold her as if
I brought the host before the altar. Oh,
she is so delicate, feather and bone,
her winged heart jerking. Her head
lies on my knitted fingers. Her eyes
are black as water. Outside I open
my hands. We hold together one
moment, breathless, then -
she lifts. The light is rose
and silent. On Tuesday
they heard tapping on the hull. Oh,
love of God,
that passes all understanding

Taking the Blame

Robert Wynne

There's something the devil wants us to forget: Hell
Only exists if we believe in it. Luckily today I don't, and I
Gather strength from the shapes of clouds. Sunlight becomes a shiv
Only God could wield. But why's He slicing the sky? What now
have I done?

With the Heater on

Robert Hilles

Certain sounds go unheard forever like the day our house burned
down when I was a boy and our dog and cat died inside, each cried
out to be saved but no was there to hear. The next day I sifted
through the ashes for their remains. I found only one tiny skull and
wasn't sure whose it was. I buried it behind the outhouse that sur-
vived the fire. The clay was cold and hard in my hands as I scooped
out a small grave. The skull was brittle and I had to hold it carefully
so that it didn't shatter in my hands. Only now do I think about
their souls and wonder if they could travel faster than fire and if
not did they perish too, the flames crackling long after. While I
buried the skull, my father waited in the car with the heater on.

Death of the Black Cat

Bruce Hunter

The grey cat peers from the night table and whines
so unlike him, urgent, and when I rise to feet him,
the silver tabby around my ankles, I find the black cat
laying on his side before the bedroom door,
my hand goes to his ribs, the chest no longer rises,
the body is warm, the tail still supple between my fingers.
He's died in mid-stride, returning from the birds feeding
at the front window at dawn, cat television in our house,
coming back to my wife's pillow, his heart likely,
after the months of death watch,
the vet warned us he won't come back

easily next time, but she'll try, there's a heart murmur
in the strange little creature with a shortened tail
that appeared at our door on a winter day ten years ago
and after months of feeding him,
on my birthday that year we let him in and he never left
pleased with a warm place and food, my wife's pillow at night
on my cap or coat, sometimes even my keys.
A lost cat has found us
on the trail for three thousand years to the Highland crofts
from the savannas and the fires, feeding with us and following.

The tabby and the grey watch as I stroke him
and gasp, "oh no,". My wife suddenly awake begins to sob,
and from the next room my old friend Billy,
tall and grizzened, a farmer now, goes with me,
as the sun comes up,
the black cat wrapped in a towel with a unicorn on it,
burying superstition and myth in the same grave,
I hold him in his sling, his head and the supple tail
still drooping, but his eyes don't answer me.
And I lay him on the grass in a grove of black cedars
That seems always to have been waiting for this
where my family buried generations of dogs,
her pet duck and someone's pony.

A scene somewhat Faulknerian in Southern Ontario,
as I sharpen my spade with a file. Billy watches
and my wife cradles the black cat and softly wails.
We are childless, and these animals are more than children, perfect
and silent as children never should be.

I cut the sod and square the hole, bevelling the sides,
a perfect small grave, my wife later asks me about,
how did you know to do it,
and I can't explain, even the gravediggers I worked amongst
in the Niagara cemetery drove backhoes,
perhaps it's an earlier memory than my own I tell her
and I was a gardener not a grave digger, planting never burying
work always began in hope and despair.

Billy stops me, think it's deep enough, he says, as if I been digging
for something bigger, all my life,
watching his father the Dutch gardener,
him seven years gone now, so much behind us,
both of us still learning from him
watching, though the Ogden boys we once were,
growing up beside the railyards,
never called it spade, always a shovel,
but all I'm sure of now is the earth
between the hard metal and my hands,
carefully mounding it beside the small deep hole,
everything deserves this grace, my wife hands him to me,
and I kiss the black fellow's snout before I lower him
and she tosses in a stuffed mouse he loved,
what's good enough for the pharaohs,
is good enough for the black cat,
no tears in front of Billy, though we's both understand.

When it's done, I tamp the earth gently,
replace the sod and for weeks afterward
everywhere in the shadows I see the black cat
waiting for him to come out.
My wife says nothing, we are past the time of children
but not the time of desire or noticing,
or the need to love something
both smaller and greater than ourselves,
to pass on the lives we've lived, or the love,
whatever the reasons we choose, if we do, to have children,
seeing the joy in the lives of my friends
and their children, though they tell me
if they could do it again, they wouldn't, the words
of the blessed. To have had love, it's easy now to say,
we could have done without.

But a month after we buried the black cat,
the grave's level and only an outline of gravel
where the grass is slow to grow
between the black cedars, I come home
from travelling tired and at 2:00 a.m.
my wife wakes me, I'm wheezing like a cow and my breath stops,
and we drive to Emergency,

humid air in the windows of the truck, our town quiet,
and I lay for a long time, listening
to the woman in the next bed, crying , whose transplant has failed,
to the children in pain and I'm grateful for only this.

The doctor orders x-rays and I'm wheeled through the darkened
halls, the hazy breeze lifting my gown, the automatic doors open
one after another, and this is a small town, I will see her tomorrow
as the market or Tim Hortons, I apologize to the sleepy radiologist,
for getting her up. But she laughs
and lifts my arms around the x-ray,
and I hug the machine that stares into my heart.

It's nothing, I tell my wife, before I drift, intravenous in my arm,
we'll be fine. Until I'm wakened by her hand on my shoulder,
the doctor shows me the outline of my heart, the fluid,
enlarged, failure the only words I hear. My father and I
longest ticking of all those damn Scots' hearts,
no uncles or grandfathers in my family.

There is the banality of evil and the ordinariness of death,
as he sends me home to wait for the tests and my own doctor,
I am not afraid, this is how it happens to most of us, one day we go
and they tell us, it's time. The details suddenly don't matter any-
more.
I sit up, watching the sun rise over the house
the black cedars full of birds now as they were last winter,
thousands warming the air with their wings,
they scrabble in the eaves,
swinging down to the feeders, jays, grackles, in the trees, crows,
on the roof mourning doves.
I sleep on the couch where the black cat did,
watching the sparrows in the dogwood, and the goldfinches.

Later I go to my desk,
the form the lawyer gave me years ago for a will,
but I'd scoffed, too soon,
and I find my pen, write instructions for the work
that needs to be done
notes for the book I've nearly finished, but I've no regrets.
For twelve hours I wait, unable to sleep, but not awake,
walking in the yard I've cleared of dead trees,
opening it to the sky, like the prairies of my youth,

I'm not old, only no longer young,
and I'm grateful for the bushes I've planted,
wiegela and ferns, Nootka cedar, purple hazel and the new maples,
the green lope of the lawn towards the swans and the river.
Always I've wanted land I could die on,
though I know unlike the black cat I won't be buried here.

And I'm grateful for these hours too
until the doctor calls, there's been a mistake
something about the x-ray and the intern's inexperience,
a friend he apologizes for, I had supper with him the other night.
The way it is in small towns. I thank him, later my wife is angry,
but I'm grateful for both the news,
and the rehearsal, never wasting anything in my life,
except time, knowing that I have days, months,
or maybe years, but not forever, one day
that is how it will be
and it's a shame to waste a death or a life
and I would have it all again.

The Gift

Dianne Aprile

I.

Who does she think she is? She hears
voices ancient, insistent — always
with her life fear, like danger. Still
she spends what a man could work a year
to earn, lavishes every coin
on one small flask of Indian perfume,
rare and precious, peace giving, gold-gleaming
alabaster captured in glass. A gift,
a kindness that can't wait.

II.

Going there, she hears the voices
whispering what comes of love:
back of hand, cold shoulder, mockery.
But she can't turn back. In a home
where friends feast she finds him.

Clutching the flask above his head,
she crushes the fragile chalice —
crystal shards trembling in thick profusion,
voices rising, sharper. She sets free
unresisting streams of liquid golden light,
her gift unencumbered - a spill of extravagant,
unambiguous love
anointing his body, touching him.

III.

Worse than she expected: the clamor and tug,
the blame. Words brand her reckless, wastrel,
foolish. Slippery glass splinters make her
palms bleed; make her feel pain is her
only reward. Don't you understand? She hides
her wounds, hand within hand, licking back tears,
their pleasure — until he speaks, words opening up
like arms, wrapping her in rest. Angry voices
fade. It is a lovely thing you have done,
he says. You have done what you could. She sees
beams of light resplendent in his hair, dripping
warm from his eyelids, beading on his tongue: unbearable
brightness she cannot evade. How did she get here? By
what route did she arrive? She can recall only this —
entering the house, finding him among his friends. And, oh
shattered, the room steeped in sudden bounty,
his eyes confirming what she never suspected
— he was waiting all along for her,
knowing who she was,
wanting her still.

28

Reversing a Crater

Margaret Avison

A scrawny old man
(scarred, bowed down, hounded by
uniformed officials and
safe people afraid to meet his eye)
(was he possibly
a fugitive? certainly in seclusion he
sometimes nonetheless
had friends who came with food
and hoped to hear him rise and toast the king!)

that old old man
wrote me a letter.
How it found its way though
from the last-ditch,
vigilant custody,
and by how many hands,
I cannot grasp. And yet it
has found its way, long afterwards,
to this unlikely megalopolis.

Now I am also aged
in as peculiar a community
as his there must have been.

More than my eighty years had
wracked his bones.
Yet he writes
forceful and drastic words with
the clarity of sealight over high
sheltering shores.

> *Suppose that chunk, that crater-gouging*
> *comet collides with us,*
> *will you say then — with him in his extremity —*
> *The tide of joy, never at ebb, still*
> *surges through us too towards*
> *new coasts, a new completedness'?*

What he said, so say I.

Part II

God in the World

Siesta

George Whipple

for Margaret Avison

Unfolding like a fieldmouse in warm hay
while gnats negotiate the price of wheat,
I grab a little shut-eye, drown
in white delicious maranatha dream.

Parched otiose two-legged lust crazed spit,
I whisper softly to sweet ears of corn
and enter ant hill churches with a slow
sad eye explores the looking glass.

Although I join my foster mother, earth,
am pitchforked into dogbone-buried clay,
I trust my rising to the Paraclete
who mends the leaky milkpail of my soul

—as in a muddy ditch a shining frog
slowly hatches in the tadpole mind of God.

Paying Attention

John B. Lee

for Mike Wilson

We look down from the hill
and see where the small
and seemingly inconsequential swale
winters below us
and know that it is one of the last precious places
and all along the hogback
we are silent
all down the snow-loud slope
we are wordless
in the slowing of spirit
beneath the beauteous wing span
of God's best creature
riding the waves of heat

above the sun-brilliant meadow
a lone golden eagle
displays its white underwing
working the love of being alive
in the heights
and then
in this landscape
of rough-bark cherry
and larch   and the last leaf rattle of low weeds
we come upon the green hallucination
of balsam, a small stand
of colour, and the cedar hush
blind beyond the edges
and know that we are wrong
to ever call the thick dark and deep interior
shadow or shade
it is rather
an artful absence of light
as it is within pure and wordless thought
where we learn the awe
of watching wild turkeys walk
like black scraps in the far valley
and deer grazing the ripe nub of pine
under the bald eagle's flush
and the vulgar profanity of crows.
"Crows love to swear,"
my companion says.
"Hear how they curse that fellow's coming.
See there, they've set guards above the deer blow
sentinels surrounding
the racket we make breaking trail."
My friend bends down
to show the fragile downy fronds of ice rim
where the deer track
punched a pre-dawn path
and I see how cold and sunless walking
leaves evidence of its hour
how we might read the thorns
for blood spray
how on the trail of ghosts we seem
and yet in the deep available knowing of nature

it longs to reveal itself and be revered
we simply speak of eagles
and they arrive hovering
above where God is making windows
on the lake.

And I apprehend the truth of wishing
something in the poet-lonely
universe, I realize
the purpose of our being
glimpse it in how this single
solitary man
might save us all
by holding out his hand palm up and open
wherein a swamp secret sits
a single salamander, rare
small, delicate as elderberry pluck.

February 18, 2000

Crossing The Winter Fields

James Deahl

Slowly the vineyards emerge from early morning darkness;
last night's loose snow slants through them pushed by the white wind.
Dawn, and only the Mennonites are awake,
busy as wasps in winter's frozen heart.

Now orchards can be seen at the shore of the lake,
every knotted branch outlined by ice, by fresh pure snow.
After the Bible is read in the room of cold wood, the work starts
— always the work —numb hands patiently learning to love this land.

Matthew tells us we draw good from the stores of goodness within
our hearts;
and that evil is summoned from our stores of evil.
Fine grains of snow blow across the farmland.
Driven by my desire for forgiveness, I have come here.
Beside the frozen lake the dark body of a hawk plummets through cold air.

Finding the Church

Tony Cosier

All morning twisting through rubble and juniper
Brings him at last to the spot. It is not a church
To anyone but him. It is a barn,
Abandoned for more than a lifetime, with only a hinge
For a door at the side and a sliding slump at the front,
A swaybacked edifice kept by spiders and mice
With moss and a scuffle of weeds. It has peace
And mystery, and music where the wind
Catches corners. An opening in the roof
Lets light drop in a floating cube.
It makes him think of a shrine he'd imagined once,
An ice church he'd read about that the vault of a glacier
Swooped over the green of the lake. And it makes him think
Of the sites of pilgrimages, Byzantium and Rome,
Places he no longer needs now he has realized
That warrior popes and pomp and power don't build a church
But a hearkening spirit graced in a steadying time
And a rooftop yielding entrance to the sun.

Ernesto Cardenal

I turned out the light to be able to see the snow,
I saw the snow through the window and the new moon.
But I saw the snow and the moon were also a window
and behind the window You were looking at me.

tr. Russell O. Salmon

If Death Hovers Anywhere

Grace Butcher

Today, at least, the only shadows
are those of birds
in quick black, over
the silver yard, gone
before we can even look up.

The sunlit snow
on the white birch
is as pure a thing
as we'll ever see
in this world.

The sky is as thin and crisp
as the ancients always thought it was,
and of an unnameable color that, if
it came from under the ground,
men would kill to possess.

This day says
in some kind of sky-blue voice
that nothing will go wrong,
and oh, I believe it.

These colors are true: this blue,
these dark forever-greens,
this white, overlaid with
gold and silver light.

On days like this
we have no reason to grieve.
The world will wait for us
to come and see it.
We have to believe.

Names of Yahweh

Marianne Bluger

Hard rain on my seared root
you are   and lightning bolt
you're wind come
thrashing one black tree
against the light-cracked sky
you're that that breaks
apocalypse - the day
and you thick night
you are the changeless
peaks and you deep valley
torrent carving stone
you're stone that holds
all raging in you are
the raging
you the din

and you the holy
silence when it ends

Winterized

Steven Michael Berzensky

When the man who's locked inside his walls
      hears nothing move outdoors,
      he rises from his chair
on the soft carpet, gazes through the sunless
window through swirls fingerpainted by frost,
      and sees whiteness spread before him
      and realizes what he has become:

a blank sheet draped over naked branches
      a sparrow songless, quivering
      in the opaque air, one
      of the snowflakes mute on the trees of the world.

desire for a different blue

Julie Berry

in your cliff little swallow i burrow
in your swoop & veer i hang by the
blood thread that joins heart to bone
skin to feather to sky
in your breath little swallow
i'll be the part you hold

inside your shell little beetle i worry
underneath your click & polish i fold up
remembering about dark believing in
the sudden airy clatter of dry wings
with you little beetle i will be
serious evidence flying away

in your weeds little ditch i prowl
in your chicory i am the desire
for a different blue in your queen
anne's lace white among perfect
i am intervals o but let me
let me be the purple centre
we learn by heartbreak.

Clothesline sonnet

Roger Bell

The hummingbirds are emerald with love
for the new clothesline's cool bisection of plane
the twang-taut singing wire I have strung above
evening, where they sometimes settle, like rain.
Ceasing their frenetic thrum, the mad desires
of hover, flash and prod, they dart from air
to stop, gently place their feet upon the wire
and then, for what feels hours, they do not stir.
No matter how exigent the day's demand
you must desist, embrace the space you live in
you must stop your heart thrashing, learn to reside

39

to generously grasp what's freely given.
Fix your frantic eyes on what you know is best,
slow the whirring self, accept the dusk, and rest.

"Thanksgiving"

James Arthur

No one can talk to your cousin, who is more thankful
than everyone else. Or at least, he thanks the right people;

not just you, for passing the squash. After his father died,
he found God ___ as if, while walking through his parents' garden,

he lifted back the flowering eaves of the dogwood, and God
was eating his mother's chives. At the funeral, your cousin

whispered by the coffin, said I love you, and other things
sons forget to mention to their fathers. You were standing

close, and heard it all with your secular ears. Clearing away
the dishes, you touch his hand quietly, say so how is

everything? Fine, he says, like he doesn't know what
we're talking about here. But this was him as a boy, too:

ask him about anything, and he will only turn his hands
into a cup, whistling at you through a blade of grass.

Unexpected beauty

Roger Bell

The hour tired
shrugs its way home
past the grey-faced factories

but at the bridge
the sun I thought had set
blushes like the last coquette
and flushes the white birches
on the Wye River's eastern shore
vibrant pink, which spills
up the steep wooded hill
illuminates the twin spires of the Shrine

then
beating back the night
two big white birds
male and female Trumpeters
shouting their impressive love
blast from the east
and split the air
down the river valley
towards the west
towards that curve
of receding day
they have fixed
in their long vision

my heart lifts with them
extends this evening
this unexpected beauty
they trumpet
I swear I hear them say
Alive!
Alive!
so even the trees, leafless, still
the dreaming spires, the river
plunged in shadow will
believe it can come like this

achingly
suddenly
vital

earth remembers

Julie Berry

it's the legion's third annual guild exhibit
mary in her magenta-sequined pant suit tells me
the body remembers everything every cell remembers
the muscle remembers how it has always felt to lie
along the bone how it's always been
mary takes my hand
lifts my arm and waves it
like a long piece of grass and i wonder what
my grandfather's body remembers in the grave a year now
the tiger lilies back of the north filed
the feel of seeds in his hand dirt under his nails
does the earth remember his body
the bones that once walked upright
does his blood yearn for its original home
does his skin remember
holding its own between
muscle and sky?

My blood remembers the lay of the land the earth too
remembers the flesh along my bones
my feet on the path
the earth remembers the days
i moved trilliums and trout lilies
from the gully the holes i dug and filled in
the touch-me-nots the birds i heard the earth too has heard
in every shovel full of dirt there lies the swallowed chirp
the swallowed trill the glimmered night-veil of cricketsong
from hills careening across the wavering edge to sunsets memory
blurs
my body stores every cloud-shattered light-spattered moment
when a tree falls in the forest the earth hears the dark shuddering
vibration
every insect snail flower cell stores the crash in its cells
i tell you my blood my dreams my memories one day will spill out
across some great soft darkness of stored rush and crash and shud-
der into light

Poem for a Winter's Night

Robert Currie

Dark and silent the street
uncoiling beyond the lampposts.
I carry Ryan from the car,
his eyes shining
between folds of frosted scarf,
his voice muffled
by layers of wool:
    Does God live in the moon
    or in that star, Daddy?
I look up and the heavens
pulse with answers.

Paths

Laurie Smith

scratching the sunset
sharp chalk on blue formica
a silent crashing parallax

we laugh at the cavemen, the grandpas
cringing at comets,
we think we understand the sky

If I Were But a River Watching

John B. Lee

I have seen the river
fatten over the land
wide enough to drown
these low lying houses
and leave
a silt in the hollows
soft as summering
and there

in the thief of flow
our broken boats
that are not boats have come
unfixed and floated away
like startled hen lift
or caught
on the tuft of some
cow-bloat hill
where the meadow smalls
above its shade
or the elm's become
but half itself in the sun
where it is full and upper doubled
in the vanity of its own self-surround

and there, by the crop loss
where sweet corn sank below its measure
and the root-washed beans
spilt down their split sprouts and died
and there
in the fertile afterflood
in the mud-calm
by the creep of green
I see how God
might love us
little by little
how His rivers
might size our doors for shadow
or touch two sides of our pane
to carry the weight of our looking
while we are
mostly looking away.

Part III

A Prayerfulness

Ode To The Letter P

Richard E. Sherwin

This poem leaks at
the ends of its black strokes the
eternity heart
       Between its letters time stops
       looks and listens for a pulse
Doctor I am sick
with passionless passions for
everything I'm not
       The parliament of crows caws
       exile at dawn from tree tops
The pale moon forced to
perch on TV antennas
etched against the sky
       O pariahs of darkness
       the weak and old left to die

Bleak explosive sounds
the world comes singing through the
holes in your closures
       Sleeve flapping scarecrows, the straw
       bleeds on the wind like the Law
But predators wait
each on its highest twig for
the end of the twitch
       I am no better, no good
       unable to let time lie
Sabbatically
sentencing each fallow pen
to its poetry
       Without imagination
       litoral dead jellyfish
Transparent melting
blob of consciousness, all that's
left of me's my sting
       The red rash sign of the moon
       waning without come to full
I must fast for sins
I'm dying to commit if

I only knew how
       Where there's death there's hope. I plan
       the plot, alte neue man
Tel Aviv survives
despite slaphappy newshawks
flowering their beaks
       This grave moment blooming like
       the phoenix kike, the blue shrike
To the right, the one
wing counsellors, to the left
the one wing critics
       My Venus mound screaming birth, my
       self become wailing other
I have nursed these months
these years or they nursed me or
it or both or none
       Who cares as long as the breasts
       are full and the mouth suckles
What's born's born. Nothing
succeeds like success. The zen
of every moment
       That teensy prick circumcised
       you big bloody prick my eye
Sees only desire
that warm womb channel forward
and back all the same
       No wonder we are two to
       raise one angel into flight
What else and where's to
do, here where the genes take care
of changing your mind
       The lightning cracks the gap in
       the heavens the floods smash through
Coming going the
new moon behind the storm clouds
veiled until we danced
       Completing blessing, complete
       the growing beginning now
The rains have rained the
waters gone where waters go
above and below

                    Dawnless yet in lamplight the
                    streets gleam black and cold old gold
Free of snarling dogs
and cars to the synagogue
of the drunken stars
                    The world belongs again to
                    God, empty except for light
That grand illusion
we flower in creating
for lack of words to
                    Thrive in the laws of chaos
                    spinning mind and speaking flesh

An Island Where Evening Never Comes

Liliana Ursu

I left the town behind me, trusting
the road would keep its mystery
perpetually.

It is a tender, familiar spring.
The apple trees beside me voice their beauty.
Their blossoms gaze into each other
like your brides staring
into vast green mirrors
of sky. Their passionless confidence
calls to us.

Unreal green. Pure sky.
Peace runs to greet you
heralding the walls of a Monastery
surrounded, uplifted by trees
doubled by water.

At the centre of the disconsolate roar
within us—the blackbird—that
immaculate prayer.

Hymn of the Harrows

Annette Schouten Woudstra

holy the harrow
that follows the tractor
pulling open the fields
like a ripe pea pod
or a good hard scratch
across a weary back
and praise to the birds
who fly a long veil behind
to cry all the prayers
for a gentle winter.

✱ Psalm 139

(translated by Paul Quenon & Ned Rosebaum)

Adonai, you search me and you penetrate me.

You yourself watch over my resting and my rising.
     From a distance you discern my distress.

My roaming, you regard, my reclining.
     My every step you attend.

There is no talk on my tongue,
     but you know it, Adonai, utterly.

Behind and before you clutch me.
     I'm put into your hand.

So dismaying a thought - quite beyond me!
     So lofty - I cannot cope.

O, where can I run from your spirit?
     or where fly from your face?

If I pierce the heavens, you're there.
        If I lean over Sheol, Ha! – you.

If I lift the wings of dawn,
        and settle beyond the sea,

even there your hand would lead me,
        your right hand catch me.

Should I say, "Ah, darkness will hide me,"
        Then night around me is light.

Even darkness does not shade herself from you,
        and night is bright as day.

You have nursed me in my mother's womb,
        yes, you've begotten my very guts.
        You've known my depths from of old.

I praise you because I am terrific, wonderful!
        Wondrous are you works.

Your eyes beheld my budding form.
        in your book everything was registered.
        days numbered, and not one of them extra.

To me, O how weighty your trials, God;
        how steep the sum of them!

Should I book them, they'd total more than sand.
        O, I'll cut it out ... yes, I'm with you still.

If you would but slay the wicked!
        put men of blood away from me,

who utter connivance against you
        rising up to the ruin of your city

Those who hate you, Adonai, do I not hate?
        I'm revolted at those who rise against you.

With total hatred I hated them.
        To me they are our enemies.

Search me, Adonai, and penetrate my innards.
        Test me and know my anguish.

Watch for any harmful ways in me,
        and guide me in the path eternal.

A Psalm of Praise

Jeff Seffinga

Praise him among all created things, for his name is holy;
Praise his name with deafening music, with murmurs in every corner.

Let the acorn on the twisted oak sing of his faithfulness,
The wilting potted chrysanthemum proclaim his power.

Among shoes in the closet his name shall be honoured,
Blue jeans and pantyhose are dumbfounded by his glory.

Hear his name in the passing wail of police car sirens,
The jet engine scream, the dump truck's broken muffler.

He reveals himself in the scent of day lilies in the garden,
The disposable diaper tossed in the garbage professes his name.

Endangered whales sing of him in the dark ocean's chambers,
Children playing ball hockey echo his care in the side streets.

All things resound with his authority and his eminence.
Praise him.

Psalm

Marilyn Gear Pilling

This is the light
   that rolls over the rim of the world like a rogue wave.
This is the light
   that pours golden into the corners, unrolls secrets curled like
   scrolls in the drawers,
This is the light
   that fills the clotheslines of the world with smacking sheets and
   antic desires,
This is the light
   that sends the fetus head first into the birth canal,
This is the light
   that caroms off the heartwood door of sorrow,
   rousing all within,
This is the light
   that beats blankets, empties basements, spreads a life upon a
   lawn,
This is the light
   that fills the luminous green pastures with cavorting young,
This is the light
   that sends men up ladders to clean out eaves troughs and teeter
   on the ridgepoles
   of their lives.
This is the light
   that sends a woman in the woods singing-

   Dangle tin pails from my arms and tap me
   the sap you get you will set free spirit
   trapped in matter, cure baldness and
   impotence, salve the hurts between.

Pater Ignatius

Marianne Micros

I want only
to take a photograph
of the doll-like bearded priest
in his black gown and sunglasses
standing at the portal
of the Byzantine church

he insists we come in
take a tour
I won't let you leave he says
and leads us to
the enormous door
heavy and medieval
the original key
in the long keyhole

he makes one of us
hold the key
it is old   very old
he tells us
as the little French girl
clutches the large steel
object   returns it to
the priest's hands
too timid to fit it
into the imposing door

inside we hear
taped music
of Gregorian chants
see a display
of medieval objects
in a glass case

the priest turns off the tape
as we light candles
chants for us his blessing
his beautiful voice soaring
to thank God
Yorgos wipes tears from his eyes

did you understand his prayer
he asks me   it was so beautiful
he prayed for us
for each one of us
but I had not understood
had been hearing the haunting
tones   not listening to
the words

now we must visit
his garden of herbs
which encircles the church
he picks samples
verbena mint oregano,
others whose names I can't
translate   tells us its name
its uses   we must smell and
touch each one

he takes us to his house
to his room
his wife watches
from the kitchen door
he shows us his souvenirs
gifts from tourists
a t-shirt with his picture
on it   foreign coins
Mento candies

he plays for us
on his mandolin
a song sung by Greek mothers
as they jumped off the cliff
away from the Turks
holding their babies
in their arms
jumping and singing
singing this song

do you understand
Yorgos asks me
they jumped for freedom
they were saving

their children
I do not I cannot
understand

now the Pater lets us leave
our arms filled with herbs
our ears hearing his blessing
his song

I am Pater
Pater Ignatius
remember me

God Forbid

Bob Hill

Please, God
don't let me drink
this wine again.
You have provided
far too much
and I have drunk too deep.
I act funny.
I have not lost control exactly,
I walk straight enough
and the outward functions
move smoothly.
Speech and sight are well.
And I do know
my way home ...
that's not it.
It's that all the inner structure
seems to slip away.
I begin to hear things -
new voices, for example, in the street.
And I see strange sights
like dead trees tipped with green
in April.
And, God forbid, I bless people

and dogs
and even stones
if the light is right.
I see fish swim
with starlight in their fins
and the fragrance that comes to me
you would not believe.
All common things have savour.

What am I doing here
standing hip deep in water
on this moon dark night
saying songs to fish?
Such action defies sobriety.

Prayerful lies

Marty Gervais

I lie to you
try to trick you
promise things
that can't possibly
be done
After a while
I believe the lies
myself, and
wonder if you
took them all in
Wonder if you
were fooled, if
you had
the human capacity
to see through things
if you had the
naivete to
believe in the
impossible
I know you
can disappoint

especially when
you can't deliver
but why do we
expect it, you never
promised, all you
said was that
you'd be there
to sit by us
to let the fear
work its way
through our blood
that worry
was no use
that hope
was the only
ingredient the
soul needed

But how can we
believe you? How can
we trust you? What's
the point of it all?

I guess the point is
to let go, to open up
to be ready, fearless
hopeful, anxious

the singing

Misha Felgin

when I become this rain
and these dark still trees
touching their swollen buds,
I will be this soft humid night
and this golden shining lamp
by the window in a quiet room.
when I become a reflection
of the lamp in your eyes,

58

I will become you, and you
will be a bird, perched
on a naked tree branch,
a ruffled sparrow crazy with
spring, full of longing, delight.
and pain that will become this song, but
who will be the singer?

The Blue Oats

James Deahl

for Elizabeth Arabell Barney (1928-1994)

In a room of thinly whitewashed pine
the man in black speaks about release
and life everlasting beyond the grave.
As he holds the book high, he speaks of death
as a portal between two worlds;
one flawed, one perfect. And with clarity
he calls on us to rejoice, to open
our hearts to celebration and praise.

But this careworn congregation of
the tottering aged; who among them
dares view death as triumph? Who believes it?
A sanctuary window stands open;
we watch as a maple welcomes autumn
and sing a hymn said to have been favoured
by the deceased. Hours later,
on the shore of a northern lake,
blue oats clutch the fading sunlight
on the last warm afternoon of the year.

Prayer On Leaving The Body

James Deahl

O taste and see that the Lord is good.
-Psalm 34,8

These feet that have carried me
over switchback trails in Appalachian darkness
I give up; they are left in tall grass
by the Baltimore and Ohio right of way
where steel rails cut close to the orange creek.

And these legs, so useful when climbing trees,
I relinquish to a boyhood now faded
to mere memory, perhaps belonging
to someone else who lived when I did,
climbed the very trees I now think I conquered.

I also cast off this intricate machinery
that gave me such ecstasy
and three miraculous daughters;
it floats mindlessly out to sea
where the currents are blue houses of desire.

My lungs I abandon to the early morning wind
that sung so well in them I thought
its music could never end;
an opera filling a concert hall
with a new day, with light.

And yes, I even close forever these blue eyes
that just the other day watched astonished
while a plummeting hawk took a sparrow in mid-air
beside the frozen river
so quickly it seemed but a dream.

And in my dream I reluctantly
pass my hands to my children;
good hands, sturdy, comfortable
in their domesticity – kneading bread,
slicing garlic for the evening soup.

Arms, heart, that worn, battered spine;
I leave it all behind. Nothing but bones,
flesh, and the tired circulation of fluids;
things of this world. A sunrise, a sunset,
the longing in the heart to taste and see . . .

Like the Irish magus I too
pray for an old man's frenzy,
though I would turn his word to fury
and seek the goodness in creation,
not its night.

Ernesto Cardenal

2 A.M. It is the hour of *The Night Office* and the
church in penumbra appears to be full of demons.
It is the hour of darkness and parties.
The hour of my revelling. And my past returns
            "And my sin is always before me."

And while we recite the psalms, my memories
interfere with the prayers like radios and like jukeboxes.
Old scenes from movies,
nightmares, hours alone in hotels, dances, trips,
kisses, bars return.
And forgotten faces appear. Sinister things.
Somoza, assassinated, leaves his mausoleum. (With
Sehon, King of the Amorites, and Og, King of Basan).
The lights of the "Copacabana"
glistening on the black water
of the waterfront, that flows out of the Managua sewers.
Absurd conversations from drunken nights
which are repeated and repeated like a scratched record.
And the screams from the roulette games, and the
jukeboxes.
            "And my sin is always before me."

It is the hour the lights shine from the brothels
and the saloons. Caiapha's house is full of people.

The lights are all on in Somoza's palace.
It is the hour the War Councils meet
and the torture technicians descend to the prisons.
The hour of the secret police and spies,
when thieves and adulterers circle the houses
and bodies are concealed. A bundle falls in the water.
It is the hour the moribund enter into agony.

The hour of sweat in the garden, and of temptations,
Outside the first birds sing sadly,
calling for the sun. It is the hour of darkness.
And the church is frigid, like full of demons,
while we continue in the night reciting the psalms.

tr. Russell O. Salmon

Just Before Christmas

Barry Butson

Oh how I love these days
sitting after school has let out for two weeks
at my darkened basement bar, four candles
burning down, Italian red in a glass, peanuts
in their shells on the next stool.
Disk Drive is on the stereo, providing
me with soothing music at no expense or effort.
Smell of Calvin Klein drifts up from one of those magazine strips
I have ripped out and laid in front of me.
Incense of strawberry is also burning at my elbow,
                    I am alone, but visitors
will arrive over the next stretch of days
and snow will fall as lazily as a willow leaf.
As lazily as I live, God I sometimes feel I am
in a Chekhov play, worse than Helena in *Uncle Vanya*.
Everyone all over the world is shopping,
but I have done mine.
It took me twenty minutes on the phone yesterday,
                    Another year is almost over, maybe my life too.
I don't mind. I hate to see another Christmas, but
I had all those Christmases as a kid in a big family

gathered in games and gossip, turkey almost done roasting,
women in the kitchen and grizzled but good-natured men
out of place in the living room instead of barns or factories
talking sports or politics, me moving back and forth
from room to room, kids playing board hockey or crokinole,
a rare bottle of Coke in my hand, watching.
All those occasions with people now dead
cannot be discounted and I believe might even shepherd a fellow
through death's doorway a little more gently.
As for this year, I cannot tell you how happy I feel
in this prologue of poinsettias and presents.
We are a most happy race of people, Christians.

Grace

Marianne Bluger

Together we dish up
carrots
    some greens
        the steaming potatoes -

as you get two glasses for wine
I serve the meat

and where were we going do you think

what did we hope or expect
better than late spring twilight
catching the supper plates
what did we ever want
more than to be with each other

at supper - to talk
here in the holy
kitchen at six o'clock

In the Chapel

Bernadette Dieker

Kneeling before the virgin
in candlelight—
eyes closed—
the image of the curve
of my lover's back
comes to mind.
I push away the thought,
then bring it back,
What else moves me so deeply?

Flight

Liliana Ursu

A yellow parrot screams
in a black cage.
He keeps striking his body
against the bars and flies
and flies

and flies
till the bars turn red—
a flame of blood floating out, a contrail of pain
wafting into the night.

Tired bird,
dreaming of liberty, you
can hardly breathe
practicing flight between the bars.
Even the glass screams
beneath these scattered feathers
suddenly gone white.

My own unshelterable heart gets lost
from its body
in the rigorous liberty of a prayer.

Varieties of Religious Experience

Peter Stevens

We've been in Canada just four days, my wife of four months and I. During our long thirteen-hour transatlantic flight, my wife is convinced one of the engines is on fire, finding no real reassurance in the flight attendant's calm explanation about fuel being burned off, the flames stretching out incandescently in the slipstream from the prop. In spite of that fiery trail left in the dark Atlantic night like some burning bush as guide for other planes, we finally reach Malton.

Stepping out of the plane into the humid heat of a Canadian night, we are shepherded into a barn-like structure and questioned by bored and touchy customs officials, crowds of immigrants wandering aimless and bemused, voices echoing in the high corrugated iron vaults, a drone like some communal prayer of grief in an obscure foreign language. Then, after a hectic cab ride (wondering what on earth it will cost, remembering that I have only a thin wafer of dollars in my pocket), we are summarily dumped outside the Ford Hotel (and what will a room cost, I wonder, looking at its ornate foyer though we soon see it's just on the verge of seediness). After fastening the three locks and a chain on the door of our room to secure our sleep we flop onto the bed, too tired to pay attention to the strange strangled shouts and fast footsteps along our corridor. Then we eventually wake, hauling ourselves out of bed late that morning and venture out into this new world of Toronto.

We are amazed at the nervy spasms of squirrels scurrying around the rich green grass of Queen's Park, zigzagging under the lengthy shades of trees, sheltering them and us from the blaze of sun, something we've never felt before—such heat! Where is the snow? We are confused by the traffic, zipping around the park at incredible speed. We find a restaurant for breakfast and question why bacon and eggs are served with lettuce leaf and chips, called French Fries on the menu. But gradually we adjust to this newness during the next few days.

And then we take the bus to Niagara Falls where we are going to live, for I have a job teaching there. We do not have to look for somewhere to live, for the separate school board has arranged for us to live in an upstairs flat, the top half of a duplex—that's what we later learn is the correct description, an apartment, not a flat, in a duplex.

But I have never known what a separate school board is. Not that it would really make any difference, I supposed. I simply presumed that it was an authority like an English Board of Education running schools and I was a teacher and I'd been hired to teach and I had a duly signed contract to prove it.

So there we are, just four days in Canada, and our landlord, to welcome us, has hung our three small rooms with crucifixes, draped untidily with foliage. Can they really be palm leaves? It's difficult to tell as they have been withered by unconditioned air to become large straggly strands of Shredded Wheat. And here in this new place our sleep will be guarded, not by a row of these locks and chains, but by the fixed sentinel stares of plaster statuettes in gaudy blues, reds, whites and gilt.

Glowering at this decoration, her face set in grim determination, my wife says, "I'll soon have all that down!" For we are not Catholics, our childhoods formed by the no-nonsense rigours of Methodism and Congregationalism, those evangelical sects conditioning us to dismiss melodramatic costumed rituals, chanted responses, candles and statues as superficial fripperies.

But our non-Catholicism is something already noticed by our landlord, for by the next morning he has reported me to the separate school board. Not that it seems to be a problem: the director of the school board invites us out for lunch, a smiling polite man, nattily dressed, his round cheeks almost shining with a rosy red, new at the job but wise in the ways of business efficiency and survival.

While I have gone to the washroom during lunch—he has insisted I drink three bottles of this fizzy Canadian beer—he tries to entice my wife to give him my contract which she had secured in the depths of her handbag that morning. He just wants to check a few details, he says, but that doesn't sit well with my wife's suspicions so she hangs on to the contract. Not that it mattered, for the board is quick to perform an exorcism later that day, a plain, unceremonious act— I am informed I no longer have a teaching job, the job for which I have come to Canada.

Early that first Sunday evening in Canada, an unemployed teacher and his new wife, uncertain about their future, assaulted by the pervasive Nabisco smell, are doing the tourist thing round Niagara Falls. After being suitably astonished by the rush and plunge of water, we walk back and find ourselves mooching across a vast parking lot, new laid, stretching out like a black lake so we almost feel as if we're walking on water. But its dark surface somehow threatens to turn sludgy, not like the gush of foam and glass-lipped slide of the falls.

In the middle of this pristine blackness we are accosted by two Americans, the man in immaculate colourful summer shirt and sleekly creased cream trousers, the woman in a floridly floral dress. He is pudgy-cheeked, smiling, eyes black-shaded, flashing miniature suns at us, oozing politeness, insisting on announcing his name to us—Clarence. Then he asks, "Who's bringing the message, brother?"

For a moment I ponder that word he's addressed me by, 'brother.' I'd heard my father at home referring to members of his trade union as brothers but Clarence's scrupulous neatness certainly is not the appearance I had ever associated with trade union members. Then I suspect I've wandered into a spy movie, and Clarence and I are agents exchanging secrets. I refuse to tell him my name: it might confirm we're spies together, this casual unplanned encounter an elaborate cover.

Then I notice at the far end of the parking lot, a large marquee is being raised. Apparently this parking lot is being miraculously transformed to sacred ground for a revival meeting. This gives me pause. I begin to wonder what kind of country I've come to, a place that on the one hand throws me out of a job with no expression of concern or regret, simply because I am of the wrong faith, but on the other hand invites me to reassess my lack of religious fervour in a parking lot complete with drive-in sermon, exhausted prayers, hymn singing to drown out revved-up sin?

That's enough for me, for I haven't been inside a church for years, except for my wedding four months earlier. From past experience I know no angel will descend from the heavens with a stagy thunderclap—in any case I believe like the Greeks in being wary of strangers bearing messages. So I'm convinced no spirit from above will arrive to overturn the backhanded miracle inflicted on me by the separate school board to reinstate me as a teacher. So I say goodbye to Clarence, confident that I can give myself my own benediction, leaving him at the mercy of whatever messenger sets up shop.

The only times I go to church nowadays are for funerals, christenings and weddings. As most of my friends are Catholic, there I am, churchgoing, right in the middle of all that religious knick-knackery I'd been told was simply gilded fakery: statues primly robed, unsexed Barbie Doll saints, simpering virgins holding cherubic babies, thick-paint-stubbly martyrs, resplendent altars with elaborate table-settings for a minimal feast, ornately carved, polished, stolid high-rise pulpits. My ears are stuffed with incomprehensible mumbles as I bob up and down at the wrong times, watching the people around me furtively pecking fingers at shoulders, heads bowed, chins on chests, as if they're ashamed of being caught doing it, then queueing up for salvation: all they need is a little nibble and sip, mouths opening for the wafer-holding priestly fingers like fish bumping at the glass sides of their tank.

And then there are all those hymns, so unlike the roustabout hallelujahs that rang out with Methodist intensity during my chapel-going days of boyhood. These hymns I hear now seem to drown under the profundo swell of the organ, the church filled with an almost banshee sound from those soaring fat pipes—surely the organist is playing all the keyboards and foot-pedals at once. I don't recognize any of the tunes so I can't console myself with a good sing. It makes me want to leave my pew and go to blow out all their votive candles, their prayers and vows guttering down to smoke, curling away to nothing like the engine flames my wife saw during our flight, that bright flare sliding away into the black night in the slipstream. So here in the church, candles blown out, the congregation would be left to flounder in the dark—but why is it that the sun is always determined to shine, making a bright spangled kaleidoscope of stained glass.

This is so different from the Methodist chapel of my boyhood. Come with me and we'll climb up the narrow front steps through two plain-faced doors into the main hall. It has a bare wooden floor—we don't go in for kneeling—straight-backed hardwood chairs to keep us as upright and uncomfortable as possible in the presence of God. The pulpit is a flimsy lectern almost shipwrecked by the weight of the Bible on it, and the harmonium, its slightly warped wooden frame seemingly scarred by the claws of birds scrabbling for worms deep in the grain, is played unmusically by a fat man slithering and bouncing on the hard bench. His thumping chords and squealing splay of fingers make that old harmonium sound as wheezy as a consumptive. The only concession to colour comes from a couple of vases of yellow tulips standing on the crisply starched linen of the altar, a simple trestle table at the front. Diagonal stripes of dull blue and grey are slapped across the back wall like a bargain carpet hanging in a cheap furniture store. Now, there's religion for you, flesh and the devil ostracized, or at least stripped down to the bare bones. You can tell what the message will be before the preacher opens his mouth.

And what preachers they were, students from Bible college full of abstruse doctrine or sentimental jabber in their sermons or laymen capable of stringing words together though they were adept at stringing us youngsters high on the scaffold of sin. Jokes we made of them, the worst we even looked forward to, because his control of the service became a comic turn. We teenagers spluttered and snorted on the back row as we listened to this man consumed by his own invincible righteousness, even in matters of grammar and speaking. So we christened him after one of his spoken monstrosities: the Reverend Horange to Heat.

But however hilarious that aspirated fruit was, we gave no thought to it at the tangerine-time of Christmas festivities. The Youth Choir went into the Christmas dark to sing carols, but what snuggling cuddles and gropings snarled the words, mouths more responsive pressed against each other, more surprising, more appealing than the well-worn rhymes about baby Jesus!

Since those teenage years, I've been trying to put my faith in other things but that doesn't work either, tested, found wanting. What kind of faith can stand firm in the contemporary world of atomic bombs, serial killers, genocide, famine, plagues?

There are children, of course, brought into the world against all those odds. To see them grow, develop, emerge, learning to be who they are, all that has something to do with continuance, a sort of reaching beyond this life, even a kind of immortality.

That first time for us, we sat overlooking the city at sunrise, no bright stars above us as we looked down into the dawn haze, nothing clear, nothing defined, the sun spreading an orange cover at the horizon, purple still hanging on from the fading night. We watched this spectacle of light, afraid, but ready for what would happen, or so we thought, ready to face anything, though hoping nothing out of the ordinary would happen. So there we were, sitting in the car, the hospital to our backs, waiting until it was unbearable.

So it happened, no complications then—a daughter born, a first, a new life, reason enough for faith, we thought. And then a second, a fast delivery, no problem, so a further reason for faith.

Then a third child, trying to believe in itself, fighting for a shape all those months, a struggle to become, in secret, unknown to us but doomed from its beginning. And it had no chance, no self, and in the end, it forced itself out a little early, eager to start here with us, though we had no help to give by then. Unable to identify itself, all it could muster were a few bitter gasps, no cries, a few breaths, eight minutes, then gone.

So I lost faith again. Nothing I tried to believe in worked. I'd been reading about dead sheep on Welsh hillsides, bodies lumped awkward among the rocky screes, dropped to the ground without warning, no signs, no obvious cause of death. And I'd also been reading about those tests, Pacific blasts, cloud-drift—reason enough to lose faith again.

Nothing we could do then. Maybe nothing we can do now. And I had no faith to let me face that short-lived child. In that difficult time, nothing could help me. Why try to remember that terrible struggle to survive? Best perhaps to forget. So it was buried in a common grave, what seemed at the time a way out, a forgetting.

But now perhaps an urge to faith rises like a silent hymn and I wish I had some real remembrance, perhaps a simple headstone to visit, a marker, perhaps a tree planted so I can watch it grow, a plaque, with a name written on it, unknown all these years. Why does this come back to me now after no remembrance through these last thirty-odd faithless years of that life, lost, buried without a name, without a date, nothing inscribed in stone?

Yet now something persists. There is this remembrance I carry with me inside, trying to give it shape with these words: is this memory becoming a faith?

Somehow I measure out that life in these words though I spill them out in disbelief that they will make sense. There is still that brief life, and remembrance like this I hope may bring some consolation. Perhaps this is a prayer, though whom I'm speaking to I'm not sure, as all my efforts to believe collapse, and even all my disbeliefs seem paltry in the end.

What remains is that small racked body—a life, still living in me, part of me in search of a blessing.

A Blessing

Michael Henson

This man wears dark clothes and is,
in fact, a dark, dark, man.
I see him often on the labyrinth streets.
Always in the same black clothes
shirt, sweater, jacket
and a long, black overcoat that reaches to his knees.

These are piled, layer on layer
dark on dark
as if he had been lacquered.
And the eyes so wide!
And the brows so wide and startled!
And the dreadlocks to the shoulders,
a frozen waterfall of intricate hair.
He is multi-layered and mysterious as a rare onion.
Day by day,
I see him mumble to himself,
or count verses
one by one
down the pages of a leatherback bible.
Sometimes I see him stand
crucified to the cold air,
nailed palms and feet,
by the cold hammers of winter.
Holding vigil in the street,
he could be a crow in a mid-winter field.
Dark, against the bustle and fog
at the windows of the laundromat
Dark against the press of buyers and sellers at the market
Dark against the leaning, sad prostitute
Dark against the dope boys in their bright coats
and the gold at their necks.
Dark as a scrap of night
blown into the street from yesterday's news.
Dark as a congress of crows.
Dark as Mister Death.
And I think he tells me not to fear such a dark,
For today, I see him and he is, again,
so like a crow in a mid-winter field
for his hands, folded to pray,
are in the shape of a beak
and he pivots at the hip like a crow
who pikes at a kernel
or a bright silver grub.
Again and again he bows
before the ark of a broken covenant
swaying like a censer in the tabernacle streets
He bows to the four corners

to the traffic
to the prostitute
to the dope boys
to the women folding laundry
behind the curtain of fog.
I slow to pass him and i raise my hand.
He smiles
with a smile of crucified ecstasy
and bows toward me also.
Suddenly, blessedly, I am in his crazy prayer.

Part IV

An Odd Theology

Theologians Never Ask the Obvious

Robert Wynne

"When God created everything,
  what did he stand on?"
                    Meghan Pool
                    6 years old

In first grade, He told me
He named Himself God
because it was the perfect word
to practice penmanship. The 'G' twice as big
as the 'o'. The 'd' a backwards 'b'.
I mastered the art of writing
between big solid lines with taller letters split
in half by faint dashes. I knew
God preferred No. 2 pencils
and pink erasers that had not yet dulled
to trail grey streaks across the page.
God was in first grade with me
answering all the questions the teacher said
were stupid. He wasn't in second grade.
Before He left, He passed me a note
that said "YOU'RE ON YOUR OWN"
in perfect print. It was a message
I would not understand for years.

Adam's Rib

Robert Hilles

Why did it start with a rib? Why not a shin, or an elbow, or toe, or
finger, or even ear lobe? I suppose it had to be something bounti-
ful, something near the heart, something hidden, something
replaceable, something that protects. Why not a lock of hair≤that
would hardly hurt? Why didn't Eve come first? Why was Adam
made out of dust and Eve out of bone? Why weren't they both
made from a single breath?

Adam awoke alone to a noisy Eden, his head buzzing with sounds he couldn't name. Did he feel lonely as he wandered a place filled with everything but love?

God made Adam out of Eve too and both earned the voices in the head, the echoes there that God couldn't feed, that made him vanished, even wrong—forgotten for hours at a time. Eve and Adam sat together eating apples and watching clouds mark the unused sky.

I try to imagine God holding up that curved bone, examining it in the light. Did he already see Eve in his mind or was he expecting someone else? Did he create her in his image or from what Adam could not take in? All the other animals were partnered but not Adam. Did God at first want him to walk the earth alone moving from place to place without anything to really do? Without Eve, would there have been a purpose to any of it?

There were only two trees there. The tree of life and the tree of knowledge and Eve chose knowledge. She led the way out of Eden, straight past a surprised God. They chose to flee, to be admonished, and Eve chose it because she had Adam's rib. He must have had hers too exchanged in that moment when God took his, replacing it with hers. Once they fled Eden they lay at night watching the stars and touching each other's ribs feeling for their hearts. God had never heard them, deaf to such sounds. He walked away as their hearts marked off the day fearing he'd forgotten something, but he wasn't sure just what. Did he sense it when he reached into Adam's chest? Did he feel that pulse distributing blood? Did he stop for a moment and check his own quiet chest? Surely he must have seen that he got it wrong then. That Eve must come first, and when he reached inside Adam, he was placing her rib there and taking one of Adam's. He laid Adam's rib by Eve's side and walked away and the serpent curled around that bone to show Eve that God could lie, could make a mistake. When she bit into the fruit she smiled knowing nothing had changed and when God came back he wouldn't notice that Adam's bone was not where he'd discarded it but in her hand. The same hand that held the fruit. He was too busy changing the rules.

Adam knew it wasn't his bone that created Eve still he listened to God and for the first time he was afraid, felt lied to and listened to

76

all God said his eyes wide open seeing for the first time that God's chest was empty, silent and he had to stop himself from reaching out a hand to touch that cold spot. As he looked over at Eve, he sensed that she thought the same. In his skull, his own heartbeat drowned out some of God's words. God could not make them understand or see. They were different creatures from him, not the same blood, not the same bone. Perhaps if he'd used his own rib and not the clay it would have been different, but as it was, he drew something out of the earth that he hadn't put there, gave it life and walked away assuming he'd done nothing wrong, hadn't made a mistake and by the time he laid down the rib next to a sleeping Eve everything was out of his control. He stepped back into the shadows listening for a sound, any sound at all. There was none. His body completely silent drifted in time but forever stood still. Without a heart to wind him forward, he was caught like a stopped watch forever showing the same time. He watched Eve sit up and speak to the serpent and perhaps he reached out a hand to try and stop her, perhaps then he knew he was powerless that it was beyond his will, anyone's will except time itself metered out so exactly, each beat caught inside a bone somewhere throbbing quietly out of God's reach, nothing in his chest keeping time.

Faith, 1998

Barry Dempster

On Christ's 1,998th birthday
I was under house arrest, on my knees
amongst piles of giddy packages
(*To Daddy, Love from All His Little Elves*),
tied to a rapidly dying tree
by stale strings of popcorn,
forced to sing along with Streisand
and her unearthly *Silent Night*.
Any wonder I felt like dashing
out into the snowy street, bare
feet as white as sheep, chasing down
the whole bloody sky star by star.
In 1845 Sir John Franklin
trailed what he thought was a longspur.
At that point he wasn't thinking

about ice or apparitions.
It fluttered, wings silvery like tinsel,
he followed, faith, a wise man turning
into a statue with every step.

Most bad days, I seek everything
I can find, from the trickle of maple sap
dripping into last year's fallen leaves
to the blur of blue light as the stranger
I'm staring at looks the other way.
If that's me tailing you down a dark street,
feel Christ-like rather than afraid.

This Christmas, I plan to steal
some straw from the reindeer display
on my neighbour's frozen lawn, strew it
by my fireplace like a welcome mat.
Forget Santa and his cookie crumbs.
Even Mom and Dad have slowly turned
into ghosts, the opposite of statues.
There is absolutely nothing I want
but a miracle, a star swooping

down my chimney, shooting sparks
through the family room,
a fireworks of childish faith.

Christ is the Kind of Guy

Robert Priest

Christ is the kind of guy
you just can't help hurting
No matter how much you love him
when you walk you stumble into him
you push him accidentally from a window
if you back the car out
you will find him squashed behind the wheels
broken out the door - all over the grate
Christ has the kind of skin
that bruises when you hold him

the kind of face that
kisses cut
He is always breaking open
when we go to embrace him
Christ the haemophilic
even the gentlest people can't help
wounding Jesus Christ
They are always running for a band-aid
and then pulling open old wounds
on a nail
If there is a cross in your house
you will find yourself bumping up against him
accidentally
moving him closer and closer to it
his arms continually more and more
widespread as he talks
Christ is the kind of guy
who can't help falling asleep like that
his arms spread wide as though over the whole world
You have a dream with a hammer
Your are making a house
In the morning you awake
and find him up there on the crossbeams
one hand nailed to the door frame
"Look Jesus" you say
"I don't want to be saved like this!"
But then you hurt him
extra
taking him down
you pry at the nails savagely
but it's no use
Christ is the kind of savior
you can only get off a cross
with a blow torch
"Father forgive them" he says
as you begin to burn his hands

Department Store Jesus

James Reaney

May I help you? You want a Jesus?
We have a different style for each of our four
Floors, for
Example, in the basement, we stock the demonic Jesus
With the hardware and the mousetraps and the col
—chicum bulbs and the rat poison.
Demonic Jesus, yes—
As portrayed in Martin Scorsese's film where Christ giggles,
An efficient young carpenter apprenticed to his dad,
Helps his father make crosses for the Romans to use.
As portrayed in a Handmade Film bankrolled by one of the Beatles
He says: "Blessed are the Cheese makers"
And his much more attractive rival is a well-endowed male
Amiable; but not too interested in changing the world.
Named Brian.

Now, let's take the escalator
To the First Floor where you may prefer
Christ as He really was,
Classified with Kodak films, notions, perfumes,
Stationary and Men's Wear.
This historical Jesus is made up of verifiable only facts,
Of which there are practically none;
Do you know there is a serious doubt that he even existed,
But finding his grave would help.
They've just found that of Caiaphas, the Chief Priest of his time.
The archeologists are busy.
Water-walker, speed baker and fisher? Virgin birth?
We've scrubbed him clean of all that midrash rubbish
After all, can you cure leprosy, blindness and death
that easily?
Meanwhile, a monastery in Turkey has coughed up
A rather interesting Gnostic scrap with regard to
A hitherto obscure passage - Mark 1X:51, 52.
At last our suspicions about his sexuality may be
Explained.

Let us take the Elevator to the Second Floor
Where the Christ of the creeds and the New Testament
Is still available.
(Buyers not many lately)
Among the patterned china, the records for gramophones.
The furniture and dining room suites,
Now this model was born to a Virgin, raised the dead,
Often corpses not so recently deceased,
Bent reality with his magic, died,
Then like Snow White came alive again:
Dared to be a crucified wretch on cross;
Somehow destroyed and renewed a large empire,
Is, no doubt, our only hope for translating us out of here.
But you know, we got a lot of returns
And customers asking for something really true this time,
Not so exciting and poetic: more real.

A man who walks on rain
Is too great a stretch for their brain.
Others say they are more than happy, but you can tell
They're not by the funny look in their eyes,
And, of course, we provide a booklet, one of many,
Just in case your difficulty is say, the Ascension,
Speaking of which, let us climb these stairs
Up to the roof of this Department store.
On the roof of this Department Store
Having a cigarette on his break,
I saw a young floorwalker
Leaning against the elevator shaft.
By the sudden flash, I recognized Him,
Yes, by the momentary glimpse
Of the Nailmarks
On his hands.

Last Suppers in Texas

Linda Frank

(a found poem)

Two T-bone steaks, lettuce and tomato
salad with egg and French dressing,
rolls, french-fries with ketchup, whole-kernel corn,
five soft tacos, angel food cake, a pint of white-
chocolate ice cream and a six pack of Pepsi
John Moody, executed January 5, 1999

Six pieces of French toast with syrup, jelly
butter, six barbecued spare ribs, six pieces
of well-burned bacon, four scrambled eggs, five
well-cooked sausage patties, french fries
with ketchup, three slices of cheese, two pieces of yellow
cake with chocolate-fudge icing and four cartons of milk
Richard Beavers, executed April 4, 1994

Pork baby back ribs, hard-shell tacos, corn
tortillas, french fries, salad with ranch
dressing, red and green chili sauce,
jalapenos and tomatoes boiled
with garlic, root beer and chocolate ice cream
Andrew Cantu, executed February 17, 1999

Four fried eggs sunny-side up, four sausage patties,
one chicken-fried- steak patty, one bowl of white
country gravy, five pieces of white toast,
five tacos with meat and cheese only, four
Dr. Peppers with ice on the side and five mint sticks
Charles Tuttle, executed February 17, 1999

A heaping portion of lettuce, a sliced tomato, a sliced
cucumber, four celery stalks, four sticks of cheddar
cheese, two bananas and two cold half-pints of milk
Frank-Basil McFarland, executed April 29, 1998

Nothing. (Though at the last minute ate a hamburger
at his mother's request)
Delbert Teague, executed September 9, 1998

Eucharist. Sacrament.
Jonathan Nobles, executed October 7, 1998

Justice. Temperance. Mercy.
Carlo Santana, executed March 23, 1993

Prime Mover

Maurice Manning

well what happened was
somebody started an engine

which got everything else
started and turning more

or less clockwise like an ox
with gears this engine was

the engine that made everything
which means all of it until one day

everything had at last been made
that was going to get made according

to the agreement which included crows
and shades of crows and everything

to do with crowery and every
thing under the sun including beams

and heat and the sun itself so mighty was
the engine so everything goes back to the engine

without which there would be no numbers nothing
to count and no little questions to answer either

and we wouldn't have anything to do with our fingers
except point them vainly back at our accusers

Nuevo Laredo, Mexico

Dorothy Mahoney

this is the market of pounded tin
framed mirrors
lanterns shaped like
church incense burners
hung from chains
light meant to pierce the darkness
with tiny splinters.

there are pounded images
of hearts and feet
small icons of supplication

the stalls are stacked
with brightly coloured things:
pinatas and paper mache fruit
pink Christ-figures crying
next to sunflower plates
T-shirts with sport logos
or crude English sayings

then there is the heat
quenched only by Corona
and small limes.
dead cockroaches pay
homage to the sun
cast to the curbs of
the main street
where myriad signs
advertise:
DOCTOR,
DENTIST,
All Scripts Filled Here
and smiling men try to sell
diet pills
beckon to follow
like hustling prophets
that can save you from yourself

this is the place of promise
a bridge crossed for a pittance
a thirty-five cent toll
and no need for pesos
printed signs assure:
We take American dollars here
the bartering is honest, for
you are always the first sale of the day
no one else's prices can compare
you are only offered the best of wares
top quality
no one has finer junk they swear

this is the market of miracles
gaunt faces attest to the poverty of pain
tourists with plastic shopping bags
try to convert
spilling small coins into smaller hands
a thin boy in a baseball cap
sits wedged in a wheelchair
watches orange and lemon butterflies
flickering over a gutter near the stalls
waiting while his family barters for tin

close by
A Mexican girl in a starched white dress
stretches her arms as if blessing
so many bound wings

The Chair of Angels

John B. Lee

for Brother Paul Quenon

The Shakers
made their brooms
from cornstraw
stalwart enough to sweep
the stars away

and yet
the dew-wet webs
that draped the fences
like beaded purse skeins
stayed their strength
small spiders spun
between white boards
an iron beauty there
to catch the light
that sleepers cannot see
though saved for them
by tiny flaws of mayfly fate
in a crush of ragged wings.

And these Shakers made such chairs
so strong and briefly perfect
that the angels
might alight
upon them, weightless
as the hollow bones of birds.

One time, entire yards
of Seraphim came down
to walk the lawns and watch
while looking out the windows
from their work
the craftsmen
spokeshaved to an awe
so gnurled it fit the dove
like buttermelt
and all the heavens
were a sheet of light...
"come in," they said
"sit down"
and every chair
went brilliant in their hands
and welcome
was a simple breath of wings.

August 26, 2000

Reading Revelation

Sarah Klassen

1.

I am reading Revelation, that exotic text
teenagers in my Bible study fall in love with.
Tell us when the world will end, they say. Let's
find Armageddon on a map. Let's finally locate it
in the middle east. What can it mean,
horns on the dragon? Was Hitler antichrist,
is it Saddam Hussein, Milosovic, should we
be looking for another?

Even those weak in math take pleasure
letting the numbers slide
smooth as honey from their erotic tongues
one hundred and forty-four thousand
six hundred and sixty-six
sevensevenseven.

2.

The white horse in the apocalypse means death,
the red and fiery one, war, in which the young
who die by far outnumber the old.
Black is the colour of hunger that ends everything.
And the last is a pale horse.

But today I'm reading Revelation
in a new translation,
the inclusive language lucid,
poetry amazingly intact. Imagine
my surprise finding the fourth horse
in a revised apocalypse
rendered pale green.

What's going on? Has this horse eaten too much grass?
Have pranksters brushed green paint capriciously on flanks
and back and belly? Has plague turned it green?
Was the translator a believer? Did he mean emerald
or jade, olive or avocado? Can green be more
than metaphor? Will this horse die?

3.

When the seven angels have blown
their seven silver trumpets
and the candles in the seven
golden lamp stands flickered out
while a lamb with seven horns is led
to slaughter and seven more
angels tip their seven bowls
until the last drop of wrath spills
seven plagues upon the world then
who will teach us how to break
the seventh seal who will unfold
like angel wings
or pages of an arcane book
the echoing unplumbed silence?
Who?

He Couldn't Fix The Tractor

Marty Gervais

I take the highway
that runs past the tiny house
near the gas pumps
I mouth a silent prayer
for my mother who told us
about summer evenings
when her uncle the faith
healer stopped by, the
Studebaker turning into
the drive his neatly cut
pants the jacket, the lapel
bursting with a rose
his smile broad and the
hands, the slim delicate hands
of a man of prayer scrubbed
white pink, the hands
that brought him money
and fame, the hands that
brought hope to

French families in the flat
lands of Essex County
My mother told me
he used to bound in through
the side door, bearing gifts
his eyes blue and penetrating
as they drank in the scene
in the big kitchen where
the men gathered at
noon, tired from chores
and her uncle would start
talking, the words that
would make the men forget
the fields, the work outside
forget the mortgage, the broken
down tractor and the hired
hand who waited by the
cement silo, waited for
the others to come
and my uncle would talk and
talk and talk, words of
hope, of God, and Christ
and Holy Ghost, of
Satan and Evil, of the broken
down tractor as a sign of
a contract broken with the
land with God and now it
was time to atone and the
men would listen to him
reaching as they did for
a pipe or chewing tobacco
as the afternoon turned
gray and cold, as his words
turned their thoughts
back upon themselves
and then he'd stride out
to the Studebaker parked
in the yard under the elms
and he'd still be talking
and that's when my mom
asked if he could fix the tractor

that stood still in the field
like a stubborn mule that
wouldn't move, and he knelt
down beside her __ she, being
all of six years old __ and he
said, "Honey I can fix bones
and muscles. I can fix fevers
and gout. I can fix bad eyes
and twisted limbs ... But
I don't know a damn thing
about tractors __ that's for
some else ... Man made
them!" And with that
her uncle swung open the
large shiny door of his
Studebaker, and wished
them well, said he'd pray
for the tractor ... That's about
all ... I think of him
and my mom that day
in the summer, maybe
it was 1924 ... Imagine
her standing on the bottom
step of that porch at the side
and her uncles big car
sprawling in the summer sun
and the hands that couldn't
get the tractor started

the word

Misha Felgin

To Martin Buber

at this moment I can say
god
to an empty medicine bottle
forgotten on the night table,

to a piece of used dental floss - -
a green arabesque imprinted
on the gray carpet,
to a little pale shadow hiding
behind the idle ceiling lamp.

I extract sacrificial lint
out of my divine navel
and blow it from my palm
into the waiting air
where the godhead in dust specks
dance in the oblique sun beams
that penetrate the blindsin
my sanctuary-bedroom
where I say Thou.

Poor Man's Heaven

Steven Michael Berzensky

Give me shabbiness.
Threadbare carpet,
remnant preferred.
Armchair without arms
and one boot
to hold up one broken leg.
Holes in a pair of mismatched cushions.
The window patched together with tape
plus the back pages of last year's newspaper.
The door that creaks on its one good hinge
and the cracked ceiling leaking raindrops.

And don't forget among the dust
the pint-sized refrigerator in the corner
with fingerprints where a handle should be.
I lean my wooden chair against the fridge door
to keep it closed.
Atop the fridge: an electric hotplate
with one pair of burners.
Only the left burner works.

at least fifty percent reliable.
I always start with things
on their last legs.
They don't spoil me
or use up my smudged currency.
And when they break down completely
and pass to the other side,
I simply give them
a decent trashbin burial.

Good old steam radiator
knocks its greeting.
I boil potatoes on the hotplate
in my lopsided aluminum pot
and brew yesterday's dried out teabag
in the recycled leftover water
Greasy, yes, but ah, still steaming.

Feeling perfectly at home,
I thumb through last year's
secondhand monthlies,
pretend they're fresh
as next month's. Then,
finished thumbing, I slip
under my shivering surplus blanket.

Scent of my warm body
takes over at last.
My own stinking skinbag
of semi-precious bones
snoozes sure as servants,
for I do not wish to sleep
the restless sleep of kings.

There's no likelihood of losses
to disturb my dreams
Deep in my scarred ribcage
I know luxury has purgatory
written all over it.
What is hell for the well-to-do
but my heaven in disguise?

Everyone wealthy leaves me alone.
That's the way I've learned to live.
Forgotten as flotsam
and at peace outside
their precarious prosperous world.

Small Martyrdoms

Rienzi Crusz

Lord, let me pass
   the sackcloth and ashes, the body
that must be whipped
   for the skin to flower
like a bloody rose.

   Refuse the saffron robe,
the Capuchin cowl,
   those ancient fakirs
who would walk the fire, find God
   in some cold bare mountain cave.

Don't talk to me of martyrdom.
   Not with my low threshold of pain,
the fool in my head, that beldam hunch
   of the coward. Yes. Peter was impressive
in death, squinting at the gates of heaven
   from his upside-down bravado
on a Roman cross.

   So, settle for less?
Small martyrdoms
   from boredom's ugly progeny,
ordinary chores,
   common and necessary as breathing?
I mean dirty dishes,
   chapped hands, fingers
that would scour the pan's dark belly,
   wade daily through Sunlight foam
like some post-prandial penance.

like some post-prandial penance.
I'm moved
from wall to wall, arching,
   turning, seeking the dark corners,
the vacuum's roar
   about my ears, an arthritic wince
invading my face.
   Come garbage day,
I'm balancing on the icy driveway,
   as the curb   waits
with civilization's broken toys,
   ichor and stink,
the "Blue Box" brimming
   for yesterday's news, Campbell's castaways,
Kellog boxes,
   flat as pancakes.

And when the snow drives down
   like monsoon rain,
listen to the crack of elbow
   as I strain at the snow-blower's starter cord.
No. I'm not smiling
   at the pain in my left clavicle,
the cold wind sneaking through my parka,
   sputter and smoke   snow-blast
that never fails to find my freezing face

Perhaps Marty

Roger Bell

(pursuant to an
earlier conversation
about my atheism)
At the corner of Davenport and Avenue Road
the bus I ride stops beside a car
whose passenger, adrift in the river of talk
leans forward so her blouse gapes
on the pale ghost of her left breast.

The fortuitious light is unusually long
the exposed breast exceptionally fine
so perhaps, Marty, you *are* right
here *is* a God
to stop the clock
let cynics gaze
in aching envy at
the word made flesh
the finely turned working
of his craftsman's hand.

Ernesto Cardenal

You cover us like the snow
of this winter morning.
I hear you in the crow's call,
the grunting of the pigs eating,
and the horn of the car on the highway.

tr. Russell O. Salmon

Tides

Nelson Ball

When I sit down in the bathtub
the tide rises.

When I get up
the tide falls.

The moon tides
the Great lakes.

God's in Heaven
with nothing to do.

Part V

God in the Cracks

God is in the Cracks

Robert Sward

"Just a tiny crack separates this world
from the next, and you step over it
　　　　every day."
"God is in the cracks."
Foot propped up, nurse hovering, phone ringing.
"Relax and breathe from your heels.
Now that's breathing.
So tell me have you enrolled yet?"

"Enrolled?"

"In the Illinois College of Podiatry."

"Dad, I have a job. I teach."

"Ha! Well, I'm a man o fthe lower extremities."

"I'm fifty three."

"So what? I'm eighty. I knew you
before you began wearing shoes.
Too good for feet?" he asks.
"I. Me. Mind:'
　　　　　That's all I get from your poetry.
Your words lack feet. Forget the mind.
Mind is all over the place. There's no support.
You want me to be proud of you? Be a footman.
Here son," he says, handing me my shoes,
"Try walking in these.
Arch supports. Now there's a subject for poetry.
Some day you'll write about arch supports."

Acolytes

Dale Ritterbusch

On Sunday we help each other
with our Lutheran robes, joke about drinking
warm communion wine
breathing red as blood
next to wafers on the silver tray.
And this week is the hard one—
fresh candles high above the altar;
it would be weeks before they'd burn down
low enough to light, easy, within reach,
and so we stand holding the flame
far above our heads, guessing at the wick,
feel that palpable Christian impatience
in faces of the congregation; my brow sweats
amid the stares, but you get lucky,
and the low flame holds.
Relieved, you wait for me as stern church fathers
confirm my uselessness to God. And God,
what must he think of my inability even to light
this simple ivory candle tipped with gold?
All my life now I feel God's impatient stare:
I get so little right, and never the first time
through, everything always just beyond reach
a candle's length away.

Bones of Desire

Paul Quenon

This manna in the desert
    is leftover from a party elsewhere!
I'm too grateful at scraps
tossed out from the Master's table,
It's better than nothing, I say,
But I hardly finish a six-pack and stuff the carton
    before I lie down on the porch and forget where I am.
Even a banquet of wine - what is it without music
    and the whole graceful company?

The saint rises, crouches at Master's door and
   whines the whole night long.

⋄⋄⋄

"Come away, O my dove, in the clefts of the rock"

        This mumbling old man -
           you call "beloved? fair one?"
        He makes the whole room smelly!
        All your roses and lilies are bouquets
           for an invalid.
        Let him stew in his content.
        Forget it. You're a
           singing telegram at the wrong address.
        Go describe your mountains and caves
            to the travel agency.
        There's nowhere for this one to go:
           if he ever leaves this shack
           it will be feet first.

        ⋄⋄⋄

"... leaping upon the mountains, bounding over the hills - my
beloved is
like a gazelle or a young stag, look, there he stands behind our wall
... "

I got lost coming here. I pushed through brambles,
   my hair is tangled, full of leaves.
I couldn't think where I was, only where I wanted to be -

Don't call me romantic! Open up.
It's dark and I'm bleeding. Honest!

\I don't care if you're not decent,   \
   \ who said you ever were? I deserve\
a little decency myself, don't I?
Do I have to break down your door?

        ⋄⋄⋄

101

"I opened to my beloved, but my beloved had turned and was gone"

So once again the open door stands empty!
      I was already afraid of that
        as my grip on the knob slipped.
      So was it written, as old as the blues -
        always the same tedious
                    disappointment.

      Last time I went raging through the streets
        until they had to stop and beat some sense into me
      - the practical types: "Stick to your cooking.
      Say your prayers.   Study some theology."

      I paid for the favor
        and lost the shirt off my back.
      Next time I'll kill myself!
      Let him make one more pass at coaxing me up again.

      I tell you I can't stand here
        and stare at an empty door.
      It happens every time!
      The empty door stares back at me.
      I can't go out, I can't stay in,
      I don"t want to talk about it -
        who wants to hear?
      I don't even listen to myself anymore.

      One thing I can count on for sure:
        it will all happen over again
      And it won't make any difference.
      It makes me older every time and no wiser.
      It isn't even dramatic - that's no more
        than a pretense.

      I'm not ready for this!
      Why can't I let it sleep? curl up
        and be like I never was?

The Christ of Velazquez

Miguel de Unamuno

In death what are you thinking, my own Jesus?
Why is your brow hid by the night-dark curtain
of you Nazarite's hair, so dark and copious?
You look within yourself, where is the kingdom
of God; within yourself, where the eternal
sun of the living souls breaks into dawn.
White is your body, like the shining mirror
of the life-giving sun, the light's true father;
white is your body, like the moon that wanders
in circles, dead, around the earth, her mother,
our tired, roaming earth.
White is your body, like the shining wafer
which in the sov'reign night graces the heavens,
the heavens which are black as the black curtain
of your Nazarite's hair, so dark and copious.
   For you, Christ, were the only
Man who dared perish with his full consenting
and thus you conquered death, which by your dying
was raised up into life. And since that moment
that death of yours became for us life-giving;
through you, cruel death is turned into our mother;
through you, cruel death becomes the sweet protection
that sugars all the bitterness of this life;
through you, the dead man who remains undying,
white as the dark night's moon.
Life is a dream, my Christ, and death is waking.
While lonely earth still dreams, the white moon watches;
the Man on the cross watches; while men dream.
The blood-less man still wakes, as white and shining
as the bright moon that shines in pitch-black night;
the man still wakes, that all his blood gave gladly
so that people might learn that they are men.
You're the savior of death. Your arms you open
to the night that is black and, ah, so lovely
because the sun of life on her is gazing
with his fiery eyes; for 'tis the bright sun
that made the night so dark, and passing lovely.
And lovely too, the solitary moon's orb,

the moon so white amid the star-strewn night sky,
a night as black as the cascading curtain
of your Nazarite's hair, so dark and copious.
White is the moon, as white as the Man's body
stretched on the cross, the sun of life reflecting;
the sun that never dies.
    Master, the moon-beams of your gentle radiance
guide us through this world's night, our souls anointing
with the strong hope of an eternal day.
Fond, tender night, mother of gentle dreaming,
sweet night, mother of hope,
the soul's dark night, in us you nurse and foster
hope in the saving Christ!

Funeral

Al Purdy

The preacher called beforehand
to make sure God
occupied a place in my heart
or somewhere nearby
I made a mistake told him the truth
said I wasn't religious
During the funeral chapel sermon
called a eulogy by some
among my mother's friends and relatives
dressed in their black Sunday best
and the smell of sweat and formaldehyde
he preached the evil of unbelievers
clubbed me with cliches
stunned me with Job and Jeremiah
hammered me with the wrath of God
and surely goodness and mercy would not
follow me all the days of my life
At first it was exhilarating
being so furious
first the grey cold anger
then relief that it took a phony god
to make the bastard possible

then amusement that my immortal soul
was worth twenty minutes only
as the red-faced prick thundered on
among roses and carnations
for his audience of one
and the dead woman listening

Getting Close to God

Robert Priest

Perhaps you want to know
the agony of the starved
the horrible ecstasy of those
closest to God.

Perhaps you want to get as close to god
as the child in the jungle
the child with the belly bloated
like a Buddha

Perhaps you want to be blasted to bits
baked in a bomb blast
You can almost see god's eyes then
a kind of grace enters you
a temporary ecstasy.

We must examine god
in all the positions
we have to know which way to point
where to pray to-
Do you ever find him in the eyes
of dying soldiers:
on both sides, behind the rocket launchers
the ancient carbines
crouching in the dark
the little scared glints
in eyes?

Perhaps we must get close to the people
to get close to god.
We must take them in our arms
and then Judas in our arms
and Krishna in our arms
We must make of each victim
a passageway to divinity
We must go amongst the poor
and feed god in them
We must fatten god up in the poor

Perhaps god is starving
in us.

The Farmers' Chapel

Marty Gervais

The pickups parked in
chaotic zigzags in the
darkness, men and
women from nearby
farms here for Mass
in the monastry chapel
one man at the back
nervous as he jingles
coins in his pocket
woman fidgeting
with an umbrella
trying to smooth out
its damp contours
like my grandmother
who used to run her
hand over the table
cloth, feeble hands
flattening out the
creases, a man clearing
his throat and someone
else turning about
in his direction, and

the man stops for
now anyway, a woman
staring at her shoes
and finally reaching
down with a piece of
tissue to wipe away
some soil from the toe
Mass at 6 a.m.
I had raced down
to the farmers' chapel
watching the lightening
break over the rounded
hills, hearing distant
thunder and noticing
the farmers' pickups
turning into the lane way
the lights rigid and
swinging out over
the tall grass — and
my sudden shadow
looming large because
of it, and there I am —
I thought — like
a boy again on the way
to the winter chapel
of my youth to serve
Mass for the old
Irish monsignor
There I am again —
this time cursing the
morning darkness, or
the wine — too much
of it from the night
before — There I am
again at the boarding
school in Northern Ontario
hastening to Mass
—flattening out my hair
doing up the buttons of
my uniform — always
rushing some place

But there I am —
the farmers and their
wives in the chapel
their caps on the seats
behind them as they sand
and pray this new day
their thoughts like mine
on other things, things
maybe not God's and
things maybe not sacred
But what does it
matter? We quiet our souls
we shut down the engines
we sit, we clasp our
hands — we hear our
hearts beating maybe
for the first time in years
like a boy standing
in a parking lot and
suddenly looking up
at the night sky
standing there in wonder
at the speckled lit sea
of night

Soul Purification

William Robertson

It doesn't matter if you leave the door to the Xerox
room open or not, says the secretary coming back
from her cigarette and coffee, a few fumes more
or less aren't going to kill you, this whole school's
sitting on a creosote pool they don't even know
the wheres and hows and whys of, except
they build the place on top of an old lumber mill
and stuff's coming up through the floors.
I calculate how many hours a week / a year
I spend here compared to her, to that other
secretary who blew the whistle on the whole business
then went home to be sick and stay
sick.

     I see the lingering effects of old poisons
on my classes today, the Aboriginal names
no one can say are or were what they called
this town before their forbears build the mill, the banks,
the churches, how much soil you haul away,
like the secretary says, to purify it, then
truck it back, and whether that means taking
the old bones out or leaving them in. We read
Shakespeare, we read *Huck Finn,* we read
Indian stores where Nanapush, Raven, Coyote
are as exotic as Leda and her swans, who raped her,
who raped her bad, then let her fall, having had
all the fun he could have, and she bore grief, she bore
pain, and where the old BA service station sat they've
put in the school parking lot and a little machine that
turns years of leaked fuel into good soil again
while in the classroom up above people like me
pace through clouds of chalk dust waving books
of old words like Zeus, like Yahweh, like
Confucius and Wisakicak, asking can anyone
pronounce these names, see no hands raise,
then mutter Jesus, so they know I'm swearing,
then watch them settle into their familiar fumes
for the day.

Something More Miraculous

Don Gutteridge

When I was seven on Sundays
belief was as simple as the vellum
leaves of the Bible-story
I fluttered on Galilee's breeze
lurking between church and home:

> Elijah's charmed chariot
> fuelled by Kryptonite,
> Jesus cruising our lake
> for angelfish and sin,
> Jonah's whale hooked
> by Huckleberry Finn ...

When I was seven and a bit
furious in the fever that shook
me like a Pentecost palsy,
and woke, later, lucky
to be Lazarus re-alive,
I couldn't recall what bid
me back:
> water-witching Jesus,
> God's rocketry,
> or
> Huck fabled on a river

but something more miraculous
than me
> did.

The Rapture

Lea Harper

It will come in a flash
You could be walking
down a familiar street
the wheel of the world

still spinning
its blur of aces
when suddenly the sun
is a gold coin at your feet
and your body dissolves
like a snapshot
its edges curled in flame
a volcanic river
sucked back into itself

Forget the small mutinies
the vital parts
you auctioned off to strangers
Heart and sperm will return
to their respective donors
Event the dust of old bones
are swept up
in a funnel of cosmic particles
their DNA restored:
    Good as new
    with skin tighter than shrinkwrap
    the brides of christ
    mounting the torn membrane
    between self and godhead -
    Eternal flame of the burning bush
    spontaneous combustion
    and its miraculous rocket launch

From this furnace
will fall the false
teeth and beasts
the dross of bangles
and nail enamel
the flakes of pettiness
like acid rain
into a dead sea

Should you fail
to surrender the insubstantial -
whatever is held together with velcro...
to equate sex and pizza

the temporary glue of lust and mozzarella...
Retire the T.V. and telephone -
whatever stands in the way
of reveiving one true signal...

If you gaze no higher
than the bank tower
to embrace a love
greater than yourself
ignoring the question
even after the fish drown
and the birds lose altitude
and the bread on your plate
turns to stone...

when the wheel of the world
grinds to a halt
you could be walking down a vanishing street
with nowhere else to go.

Chosen People

Jeff Seffinga

Only two years in this land
I learned how we were chosen.
Skipping an afternoon of school, I hid
in a churchyard's cool shadow,
immigrant child among the gravestones
of Loyalist settlers so long dead,
and with wide yes of innocence
watched my father at work.
In sun hot as an Egyptian desert,
under the dignified architect's direction
workmen built a wall.
The high line of red brick was urged
upward by hand and trowel,
levels, and taut lines of twine.
Shouts of the bricklayers rang like bells
through the churchyard sanctuary.

My father shirtless with sweat running
like small streams in the dry dust
layered like desert sand on his back,
loaded bricks on a wooden frame.
When a builder called, he carried
the load aloft up the ladder:
a three-legged mule sent scrambling
on the cliff's steepest trail.
Or when one called for mortar
he filled a bucket, hung it from a pulley,
and with the practiced grace
of the bell-ringer at a cathedral carillon
he'd send the bucket skyward
and spill no drop.
He stood always tall, always alert
to every craftsman's call.
I knew then how the Hebrews built
those tombs at Pharaoh's will
and understood that my father believed
for himself the promise God gave them:
This shall not last. The future will belong
to your children and their children's
children, for you are chosen.

And everywhere children's voices
ring among brick walls.

Herzliyah Pituah

Richard E. Sherwin

No wind broods over
my abysses, breeding space
dividing waters
    No voice exhales its light for
    signs and seasons conception
Such seed I receive
is of my kind, a chaos
voiding darknesses
    For this I scream enough the

blessing is too great for death
And I must live it
cobbling my creations moon
by moonbeam shadow
    Dodging vampire angels in
    the flicker a leaf allows

At noon my terrors
neigh me stunned and lusting for
a soul to bear the light
    Sweating writhing begging God
    for a twin to swap me for
Sun and heart stroke's all
I ever got, that chill of
death that shivers hot
    Dogs and lions bark my dreams
    of falling backwards for good
Waking past sunset
relieved my heart is hungry
for chaos again
    Without us devils what hope
    in hell has holiness got
What stretches the mind
and lazy soul as good as
seeing evil joy
    What makes law and order dear
    like feeling itself decay
I pay the price of
flowering in freedom more
willingly than saints
    Pay for what you want, in joy
    it's not for what you don't, love
Worlds upon worlds to
wrench some room for heart's desire
from, worlds without ends
    But not for cheapskates not for
    those professionally poor

All for nothing, all
and nothing, either, both will
sweep the empty board

Stuffing your pockets with void
jingle jangling like the dove
And with our siller
at the tiller fair stood the
wind for Skye in faith
Come rain come storm our Flora
saved the good old cause for myth
Who's not shuddered there
at sunset, queasy spirits
still not settled down
It's the hope in hopelessness
as makes us cowards stand to
This last leaf scratching
raw the scab I thought time healed
and hasn't couldn't
My Israel, God's chosen
nomads in time, the trumpet
Gathering ashes
from this cornerless graveyard
to make dry bones with
Pipes and drums got life beat all
hollow, even I would rise
Against my judgment
to moonlit copulations than
lie tame in the dust
Skirling that minor whirlwind
personality precedes

Madness all to try
again again and again
that madness again
Abysses hovering un
der voids to hear such a voice
Tickling chaoses
into formlessness enough
for heavens to be
Freezing the flow to node
directions like rose buds furled
And waiting to sound
off in such light scent the song
of fires and waters

And here we go again, Lord
Serving refusing to serve

At the Support Group for Non-Believers

Robert Wynne

Ralph says the moon landing was faked.
June says the earth's not spinning.
Tim says no coffee has ever been decaffeinated.
"Yes," is all it says on the blackboard.
It's my fourth meeting
and finally I feel
I know these people enough
to admit I don't
believe them.

I pass out rolls of Cherry Lifesavers
and tell everyone
I think love is the hole
in the middle: what's important
is what surrounds it.
I'm trying to convince myself

it's like God, I say, except
He'd be butterscotch.
And when love or God
has dissolved on your tongue,
all that's left is the flavour.

You can't prove anything.

The Agnostic's Villanelle

Marilyn Taylor

Maybe disbelieving is too easy,
and something's really out there in the dark.
Go ahead, say I'm crazy,

warn me that religion drives a fuzzy
argument—a little myth, a lot of murk—
still, disbelieving seems too easy.

Take emotions. Or desires. Sleazy
aberrations? Oddball quirks
of psycho-chemistry? I say it's crazy

to dismiss it all with breezy
scorn, or credit Science with the spark
that quickens. Just a touch too easy

for us—the devotedly blase—
to claim with a smirk
a true belief in disbelief. Aren't we crazy

if we don't allow ourselves a hazy
sense of something more at work?
You'll call me crazy,
but for me, disbelieving's too damned easy.

Confessions (Two)

Degan Davis

I have come a long way
not knowing where I was going
but knowing it was to see something
I'd never seen

I have heard stories
of such light and such dark
I can't decide   God
where you're bound

A man and a woman
touch each other
only so far but live
to love further

I have come a long way
not knowing where I was going
but knowing it was to see something
I'd never seen